Searchlight
BOOKS™

What
Are Earth's
Cycles?

# Investigating

# Seasons

Orlin Richard

Lerner Publications • Minneapolis

Content Consultant: Alan Robock, Distinguished Professor of Environmental Sciences, Rutgers University

Lerner Publications Company
A division of Lerner Publishing Group, Inc.
241 First Avenue North
Minneapolis, MN 55401 USA

For reading levels and more information, look up this title
at www.lernerbooks.com.


**Library of Congress Cataloging-in-Publication Data**

Richard, Orlin, author.
    Investigating seasons / by Orlin Richard.
       pages cm — (Searchlight books. What are earth's cycles?)
    Audience: Ages 8–11
    Audience: Grades 4 to 6
    ISBN 978-1-4677-8059-9 (lb : alk. paper) — ISBN 978-1-4677-8339-2 (pb : alk. paper) — ISBN 978-1-4677-8340-8 (eb pdf)
      1. Seasons—Juvenile literature.  2. Earth (Planet)—Rotation—Juvenile literature.
I. Title.  II. Series: Searchlight books. What are earth's cycles?
QB637.4.R528 2015
508.2—dc23                                                                                    2015000962

Manufactured in the United States of America
1 – VP – 7/15/15

# Contents

# Chapter 1

# WHAT IS A SEASON?

In many parts of the world, people swim in lakes during summer. And they ice-skate on those same lakes during winter. But they cannot ice-skate in the summer, and they would not want to swim in the winter. Why is the weather so different during summer and winter?

The same lakes people skate on in the winter turn to liquid water in the summer—all thanks to Earth's cycles. What is a cycle?

These changes happen because of Earth's seasonal cycle. The natural world has many different cycles. A cycle is a pattern that repeats over time in a predictable way.

A boy jumps into a lake on a hot summer day.

## Measuring the Seasons

What is a season? We think of summer as warm and winter as cold. But suppose there is a warm day in winter. That does not mean it is summer! The seasons begin and end on specific dates. These dates are based on the position of the sun and Earth. This is the astronomical definition of seasons.

It takes 365.24 days, or about one year, for Earth to make one trip around the sun.

# A METEOROLOGIST TAKES A READING OF WEATHER-SENSING EQUIPMENT.

But not everyone measures the seasons in this way. Meteorologists are scientists who study the weather. They base seasons on the temperature at different times of year. This system does not depend on the sun's position. It depends more on the climate, or long-term weather patterns.

## Opposite Seasons

To complicate things further, seasons are different depending on where you live. The Northern and Southern Hemispheres have opposite seasons. Winter happens from about December through February in the Northern Hemisphere. Meanwhile, those months are summer in the Southern Hemisphere.

Earth's seasons affect agriculture and climate. They can even affect health. But why are there seasons at all? What exactly causes a season?

Because of the seasons, this farmer must harvest his crops at a certain time of year.

# See the Cycle

Look up the average temperatures for your hometown. Make a chart showing the temperature for each month of the year. How much does the temperature change between summer and winter?

# Chapter 2

# WHAT CAUSES THE SEASONS?

Some people think the seasons change based on how close Earth is to the sun. But that is not true. In fact, Earth is closest to the sun in early January. That is the middle of winter in the Northern Hemisphere.

Hot summer days are not a result of Earth's distance from the sun. What does cause summer's heat and winter's chill?

The seasons are actually caused by the tilt of Earth's axis. Imagine a line through Earth. It goes from the North Pole to the South Pole. This is Earth's axis. But the axis is not straight up and down. It is tilted 23.45 degrees as Earth orbits around the sun.

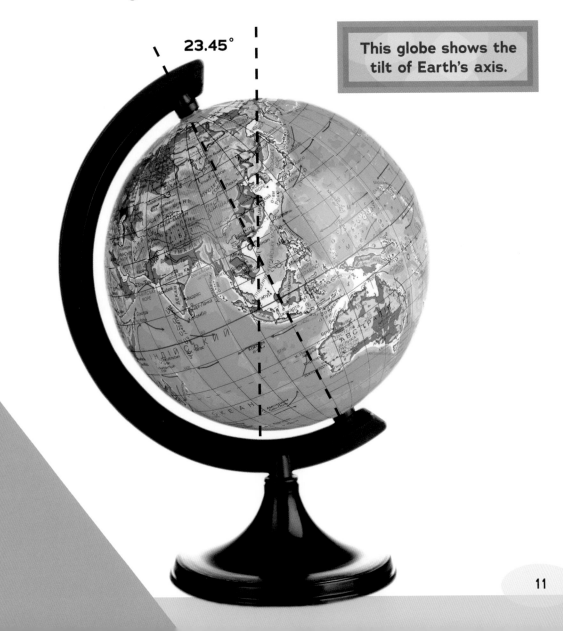

23.45°

This globe shows the tilt of Earth's axis.

The United States is in the Northern Hemisphere. Its warmest months are June through August.

## Stronger Sunlight

Earth's tilt means different amounts of sunlight fall on different places. For example, Earth's northern half is tilted toward the sun for part of the year. So the northern half gets more sunlight during this time. The extra sunlight warms the Northern Hemisphere more, making it summer.

At the same time, the Southern Hemisphere is tilted away from the sun. This hemisphere gets less sunlight, making it winter. Later, the seasons switch. Earth moves to the other side of the sun. But the tilt of Earth's axis does not change. That means the Southern Hemisphere gets more sunlight during the other half of the year.

People relax on a beach in Australia. This country is in the Southern Hemisphere, so its warmest months are December through February.

# See the Cycle

Shine a flashlight onto a sheet of paper. Tilt the paper so the light hits it at an angle. Notice how the shape of the light on the paper changes. The same amount of light spreads over a wider area. So each square inch of paper gets less light. This is similar to the tilt of Earth. This tilt causes different amounts of light to hit the hemispheres at different times of year. The extra hours of sunlight contribute to summer warmth. These factors result in the seasons.

## Solstices and Equinoxes

Winter and summer each begin at a solstice, based on the astronomical definition of seasons. A solstice happens when one hemisphere faces the sun most directly.

Stonehenge is a monument in England. Scientists think it helped ancient people predict solstices.

Fall and spring each begin at an equinox. This happens when the Northern and Southern Hemispheres get the same amount of sunlight. The sun is almost directly over the equator at this time.

## CHANGING SEASONS

**Northern Hemisphere: spring equinox**
**Southern Hemisphere: fall equinox**

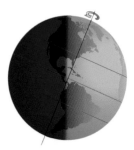

**Northern Hemisphere:**
**summer solstice**
**Southern Hemisphere:**
**winter solstice**

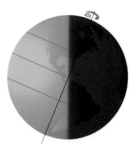

**Northern Hemisphere:**
**winter solstice**
**Southern Hemisphere:**
**summer solstice**

**Northern Hemisphere: fall equinox**
**Southern Hemisphere: spring equinox**

# WHEN IT IS MIDNIGHT IN CHINA, IT IS DAYTIME IN THE UNITED STATES.

## Night and Day

Earth revolves around the sun once per year.  Earth also spins around its axis once per day.  So different parts of Earth face the sun at different times.  This causes night and day.

In places that are very far north, the long winter nights give people lots of chances to see the northern lights.

The seasonal cycle affects the length of a day. The most sunlight strikes during the summer solstice. This is when a hemisphere faces the sun most directly. And that hemisphere receives the least amount of sunlight on the winter solstice. The winter solstice in the Northern Hemisphere is the summer solstice in the Southern Hemisphere.

# Polar Opposites

The amount of sunlight an area receives depends on how far north or south it is. Near the equator, the amount of sunlight does not change much. But the amount of sunlight changes a lot near the poles. The North Pole gets six months of sunlight between March and September. The South Pole gets six months of darkness.

At the South Pole (BELOW), the sun stays out for half the year. At the same time, the North Pole is dark.

The summer solstice is the day with the most sunlight. But it is usually not the year's warmest day. That is because it takes time for sunlight to warm up the planet. In fact, it takes about a month. So the year's warmest days are usually in the middle of summer, not the beginning.

This ice cream cone quickly melts on a hot summer day!

IN THE TOWN OF KAYABWE, UGANDA, PEOPLE HAVE SET UP A DISPLAY TO SHOW WHERE THE EQUATOR PASSES THROUGH.

Near the equator, the temperature and amount of sunlight are similar all year. These places still have seasons. But their seasons have more to do with rainfall.

# Chapter 3

# WET AND DRY SEASONS

The parts of Earth near the equator are called the tropics. The tropics do not have four different seasons. Instead, they have wet and dry seasons.

Seasons are different in tropical rain forests than in other parts of the world. What seasons do the tropics have?

## Heat and Rain

The tropics get lots of sunlight all year. This sunlight causes heat. And the heat makes water in the oceans evaporate. This water turns into precipitation, which falls in the form of rain.

There is more rain around the equator than anywhere else in the world. This rain travels in bands. When it passes over an area, it causes a wet season. When it leaves, there is a dry season.

**This map shows the tropical rain belt, a thick band of showers that stretches across Earth's tropical regions.**

There can be one or two wet seasons each year. There can also be one or two dry seasons. The number depends on how many times a band of precipitation passes over an area.

Wind affects the seasons in some parts of the world.

A monsoon is a strong, seasonal wind that often carries heavy rains with it. Monsoons traveling from the sea to land create a rainy season. This happens because the monsoon carries in lots of ocean water. Monsoons reverse during the dry season. They blow toward the sea.

Monsoons sometimes cause floods, which can wash out streets and damage neighborhoods.

# See the Cycle

Look up the monthly rainfall in your hometown. Compare these numbers to the rainfall in Mumbai, India. Does Mumbai's cycle look different from your hometown's? What does this tell you about monsoons?

# Chapter 4

# WHAT THE SEASONS DO

You know what causes the seasons. But do you know why the seasons are important? These yearly changes in the weather have a huge impact on people, animals, and plants around the world.

The seasonal cycle is important to animals. What else does the seasonal cycle affect?

## Agriculture

Farmers have learned how the seasons affect plants. Different crops grow best at different times of the year. And most crops grow better in certain climates. For example, many apples grow best in places with cold winters.

**People usually pick apples in late summer or early fall.**

Most of the world's rice grows in Asia.

Rice is an important food in many parts of the world. Rice needs warm, wet conditions to grow. So most rice is grown near the tropics. What fruits and vegetables do you like to eat? Do you know when and where they grow best? Find out!

## Seasonal Storms

The seasonal cycle affects many types of storms. For example, hurricanes need warm ocean water to form. So those storms usually happen during late summer and fall in the United States. This is when ocean water is warmest.

A powerful hurricane makes its way toward land.

## Animals

Many animals change behavior with the seasons. Some migrate when the seasons change. Birds in the Northern Hemisphere fly south for the winter. They fly toward warmer weather. Many whales move to colder waters in the summer. They travel to warmer waters in the winter.

**Humpback whales are one of the many animals that migrate when seasons change.**

**Bears often hibernate in dens all winter long.**

Other animals hibernate, or rest through the winter. Animals that hibernate include bears, squirrels, bats, and even turtles. Animals do not need much food when they hibernate. Their heartbeats and breathing slow down. This helps them survive winter, when food is harder to find.

FLU SHOTS HELP PEOPLE STAY HEALTHY DURING THE COLD WINTER MONTHS.

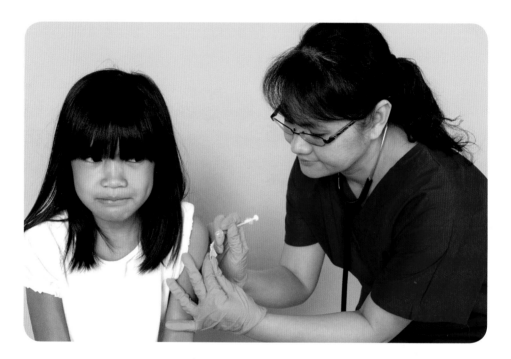

## Diseases

Even germs and viruses change with the seasons. For example, the flu virus spreads more easily when the air is cold and dry. That is why people often get a shot or inhale a dose of medicine to help prevent the flu in the fall. Many other diseases spread more easily during certain seasons too.

# Light and Power

The seasonal cycle also affects energy use. Many people need to heat their homes during winter. That means they use more energy. Also, shorter days mean people use more lights in the evening.

In the winter months, many people turn their lights on before five o'clock in the evening. In the summer, they may not turn their lights on until eight o'clock.

During daylight saving time, people do not have to turn on their lights so early. There is also more daylight when most people are awake.

Daylight saving time (DST) occurs in most of North America and western Europe. During DST, people set their clocks ahead by one hour in the spring. That means sunset happens later in the evening. In the fall, people set their clocks back to normal time.

# See the Cycle

How much electricity do you use? Make a list of everything you do during the day that uses electricity. Would this list be different during other seasons?

   Next, make a new list of ways to use less energy. How many things can you cross off the first list?

The sun shines on a nature trail on a beautiful fall day.

The seasonal cycle never stops. And the seasons affect people's lives in many ways. In fact, seasons play a role in almost everything we do!

# Science and the Seasons

You can investigate the science behind the seasons on your own! Record the time that the sun rises and sets each day for one week. To check your times, visit http://www.esrl.noaa.gov/gmd/grad/solcalc. Calculate the hours of sunlight that occur each day. Are the days getting shorter or longer? What does this tell you about the relationship between Earth and the sun?

# Glossary

**agriculture:** farming and harvesting food

**axis:** an invisible line connecting the North Pole and the South Pole. The axis is tilted 23.45 degrees as Earth orbits around the sun.

**climate:** the long-term weather of a place

**equator:** an imaginary line around the center of Earth. Places near the equator are usually very warm.

**equinox:** the day when the sun is most directly over the equator

**evaporate:** to change from a liquid into a gas

**hemisphere:** one half of Earth. Earth has two hemispheres, the Northern Hemisphere and the Southern Hemisphere.

**hibernate:** to go into a deep sleep during the winter

**hurricane:** a large storm with strong winds and heavy rain

**meteorologist:** a scientist who studies the weather

**migrate:** to travel to a different place

**monsoon:** a seasonal wind pattern that creates a lot of rain in the summer

**precipitation:** rain, snow, or other forms of water that fall from the sky

**solstice:** the day when a hemisphere is tilted most toward or away from the sun

**tropics:** warm, wet climates

# Learn More about the Seasons

## Books

Aguilar, David A. *13 Planets: The Latest View of the Solar System*. Washington, DC: National Geographic, 2011. This book is filled with colorful pictures and discusses the details of each planet.

Storad, Conrad J. *Earth Is Tilting!* Vero Beach, FL: Rourke Publishing, 2012. Learn more about how Earth's tilted axis affects the seasons in this informative book.

Waxman, Laura Hamilton. *The Sun*. Minneapolis: Lerner Publications, 2010. This title explains the effects of the star at the center of our solar system.

## Websites

**NASA: What Causes the Seasons?**
http://spaceplace.nasa.gov/seasons/en
This website is full of interesting information about what causes the seasons, including an explanation of why Earth's axis is tilted.

**NOAA: Changing Seasons**
http://www.education.noaa.gov/Climate/Changing_Seasons.html
This helpful site includes a map that shows changing vegetation patterns during different seasons.

**Seasons Aren't Dictated by Closeness to Sun**
https://www.khanacademy.org/science/cosmology-and-astronomy/
earth-history-topic/earth-title-topic/v/seasons-aren-t-dictated-by
-closeness-to-sun
Watch the informative video at this site to learn why Earth's closeness to the sun is not what causes the seasons.

# Index

# Photo Acknowledgments

The images in this book are used with the permission of: © L. Akhundova/Shutterstock Images, p. 4; © Yanik Chauvin/Shutterstock Images, p. 5; © djgis/Shutterstock Images, p. 6; © Fineart1/Shutterstock Images, p. 7; © Darrin Henry/Shutterstock Images, p. 8; © Barry Blackburn/Shutterstock Images, p. 9; © kazoka/Shutterstock Images, p. 10; © Africa Studio/Shutterstock Images, pp. 11, 34; © 2xSamara.com/Shutterstock Images, p. 12; © Dan Breckwoldt/Shutterstock Images, p. 13; © peepo/iStockphoto, p. 14; © Edward Haylan/Shutterstock Images, p. 15; © Peter Hermes Furian/iStockphoto, p. 16; © zgj23/Shutterstock Images, p. 17; © SurangaSL/Shutterstock Images, p. 18; © Galen Rowell/Corbis, p. 19; © Paul Burns/Blend Images/Thinkstock, p. 20; © Pal Teravagimov/Shutterstock Images, p. 21; © kompasstudio/iStockphoto, p. 22; © the huhu/iStock/Thinkstock, p. 23; © Caisii Mao/NurPhoto/Corbis, p. 24; © Lewis Tse Pui Lung/Shutterstock Images, p. 25; © Ross Kummer/Shutterstock Images, p. 26; © fotokostic/iStockphoto, p. 27; © kataleewan intarachote/Shutterstock Images, p. 28; © Harvepino/Shutterstock Images, p. 29; © Paul S. Wolf/Shutterstock Images, p. 30; © Andreas Argirakis/Shutterstock Images, p. 31; © Joel Joson/iStockphoto, p. 32; © Steve Photography/Shutterstock Images, p. 33; © Jeffrey Hamilton/Stockbyte/Thinkstock, p. 35; © Jiri Vaclavek/Shutterstock Images, p. 36 © Leena Robinson/Shutterstock Images, p. 37.

Front Cover: © Lilkar/Shutterstock.com.

Main body text set in Adrianna Regular 14/20.
Typeface provided by Chank.